How to Write a Book in 24 Hours

(24 Hour Bestseller Series: Book 1)

JAMES GREEN

ISBN: 150880138X
ISBN-13: 978-1508801382

DEDICATION

To my wife, family & Boo.

CONTENTS

COPYRIGHT

Contact details

james@24hourbestseller.com

Twitter: @jamesgreenseo (https://twitter.com/jamesgreenseo)

Facebook: https://www.facebook.com/jamesgreenseo

Website: www.24hourbestseller.com

1. INTRODUCTION

I want to share with you a system that will transform the way you write books – forever!

A system that will:

- provide a step-by-step, repeatable recipe for writing success,
- stir your creative juices to constantly think up new book ideas,
- make the whole writing process both easier and faster,
- show you how to stay motivated,
- produce a high quality end-product every time,
- make you more productive than ever, and most importantly in my opinion:
- make writing enjoyable once more!

Perhaps you've hit a hurdle or a sticking point in the writing process, or you're looking for a method to write your books more effectively. I can help!

Whether you're a complete novice and have never even written a book before, are struggling to come up with new book ideas, or a seasoned author who simply needs some tips on how to write more effectively, then this book is for you!

In this book I want to encourage you to get you into the writing habit; and once you do, you won't be able to stop!

I'm an internet marketer and an author. But the authoring part hasn't always come naturally to me.

I used to be guilty of saying: 'I'm stuck for ideas' or 'I'm not a writer, how can I possibly write an entire book?' or 'who would want to hear what I have to say?'; I now realize how ridiculous all of those statements were.

And whenever I came up with a new book idea, I would vaguely decide on the topic areas I wanted to discuss and then either:

1)   get my head down and start writing, or

2)   outsource the entire book.

With the first method, I would blindly tap away at the keyboard, thrashing out my ideas like some mad professor, just willing myself to complete each section.

When I finally came up for air I would then decide my topics were all over the place and then spend ridiculous amounts of time rearranging each section, stuffing paragraphs into various sections and re-writing huge swathes of text. My first book took me over three months to complete.

With the second method, I would simply send an outsourcer my proposed book title, together with a list of areas I wanted them to cover.

Yes, a book could be produced in record time, but the results were incredibly variable from the mediocre to the darn right horrific! Some submissions looked like they'd been translated from English to Chinese and then back again! And even when the results were reasonably okay I'd still need to proof it extra carefully and re-word huge swathes of text in order to give it 'my voice'. I was risking my reputation both with Amazon and, more importantly, with my audience.

I also found neither method enjoyable; in the first case because I found it such a chore, and in the second case because it felt both unethical and unrewarding.

I was getting zero satisfaction out of the whole process. But I knew that writing non-fiction books was a potentially hugely lucrative business. I had already proved that with the sales of my first books: my very first book, (the one that took me 3 months to write) at its peak, was selling over 100 copies per month.

If I could just find a way of scaling up and begin rolling out high quality books to a sufficiently high audience on a regular basis, I was on to a winner.

There simply had to be a better way of producing high quality books without all the headaches.

So, I trawled the internet, consumed articles and numerous books to discover how other authors were managing it. I liaised with other successful authors and scraped every tidbit of advice and technique I could lay my hands on.

Some of it worked. Lots of it didn't. But over time I slowly formulated my own recipe for producing books in record time; books that I can once again be proud of, and that I now even enjoy writing!

It's taken me a long time to refine and tweak my methods and it has undergone a fair few revisions over the years.

But I'll show you how, using my formula, you can easily create a successful, high quality book from idea to print, again and again.

And by breaking down the process into distinct, easy to manage phases and by allocating time to each, it really is possible to do this in only 24 hours!

Ok, I'm not saying you need to spend 24 hours back to back – unless you're a complete masochist.

You are permitted to break the time into bite-sized pieces; in fact, I highly recommend it!

You may only be able to spare an hour a day, or maybe two or three. But, using my formula, the whole process should only take up 24 hours of your valuable time.

And if you follow the formula, you will even enjoy the process, which I believe is absolutely paramount to your writing success.

"Enjoyment is an incredible energizer to the human spirit" - John C Maxwell

I'll also show you how you can generate new ideas and begin the writing process with an exact framework in mind, knowing that you have the right sections in a logical order and that the resulting work will be of a high quality. And as we all know, quality sells.

Why write a book?

There's never been a more exciting time to be an author.

The world of publishing changed beyond all recognition when, in 2007, Amazon launched their first Kindle device. In the beginning there were many sceptics of the eBook platform and few people could ever have imagined the publishing explosion this would lead to.

But it isn't just the delivery platform that's changed: the traditional model of producing huge 500 page tomes is becoming increasingly rare in the non-fiction genre. Your 21st century audience demands quick fixes to problems, they will no longer put up with being bombarded with reams of statistics, padded with overly-detailed and often barely relevant information.

People simply don't have the time or the inclination to trawl through piles of superfluous information to get to the solution they want.

And that's great for us as well as for the reader. We, the indie author, have arrived on our white steeds to satisfy this craving, offering fast, efficient solutions to problems as well as inspirational stories and advice!

The Amazon Model

And, thanks to Amazon, it's now easier than ever to publish your own books. Gone is the need to approach large publishing houses, groveling at their feet to ask if they will even consider our efforts; and being left with just the crumbs of profits after they extract their exorbitant royalty fees.

Publishing today is a low-risk, high reward business, with Amazon generously paying you a 70% royalty on your book sales. Yes, you heard it right, 70%!! And for their 30% cut they'll promote your book, deal with the deliveries, the refunds and all the customer service!

And with the right topic, just one book will continue to earn you money for many years to come, even as you sleep – the true meaning of passive income!

Amazon actually WANTS you to publish more and more books, particularly if your previous one was a success. And they will actively promote your wares to an eager audience 24 hours a day, 7 days a week; for nothing!

Scale it up and it becomes a seriously life-changing proposition.

A book also means that you will have an asset, an information product, fully copyrighted, that belongs to you and you alone. That you can do with as you see fit: you can turn it into a physical book, sell it on other outlets, create and sell PDFs from it, convert it into a video series, extract sections to Facebook, your website, on blogs, even as Tweets. And the list goes on!

I am an Author!

A book gives you a tremendous amount of authority and gravitas, turning you into the 'go-to girl/guy' in your genre.

And you can leverage that authority to create a following and begin a dialog with your captive audience. In turn, this can provide opportunities in terms of further sales and back-end offers.

Never underestimate the power of a book!

Fiction or Non-Fiction?

I think many people have a fiction book inside them, waiting to be released (me included!). But most fiction books have something in common: they take a lot of time!

Non-fiction books are there to provide a solution to a problem.

Choose the right-sized problem and the resultant book becomes pretty straightforward.

In short, non-fiction books are (generally):

1.   Shorter;

2.   Easier to write (information is already out there);

3. Easier to rank for, using high-value keywords, and most importantly

4. Easier to sell!

So I'll be concentrating on the non-fiction genre in this book; your fictional roller-coaster of a novel can still bubble away under the surface!

For now, let's make some serious money to fund that burning ambition of yours!

Why do I need a writing *formula*?

"Living your life without a plan is like watching television with someone else holding the remote control." – Peter Turla

Writing a book without a decent formula is like nailing jello to the wall.

It's how I used to do it.

Using a half-baked plan, I'd plough ahead, just writing as a stream of consciousness. I'd finally emerge days later only to find a complete lack of coherence with what I'd just written, with nothing flowing from one section to the next. So I'd sit down and work out where to re-arrange the text into different sections, only to find I wasn't even happy with the sections I'd come up with in the first place!

What's needed is a bullet-proof plan, a recipe for writing that can be set on full 'rinse-and-repeat' mode, that will save time, laser-focus your mind into exactly what's required and that can turn you into an automatic writing machine!

A plan for:

1. Generating new ideas,

2.   Validating those ideas,

3.   Creating a complete (and coherent) outline of your book,

4.   Writing your book effectively,

5.   Proofing your book, and

6.   Publishing your book.

A plan that not only saves you time, but that also makes the whole process both enjoyable and easy. One that provides a complete framework that we simply need to follow along with, where each step leads logically to the next. Once that's in place your book will almost write itself!

I used the exact same formula to write this book in less than 24 hours.

You may not hit this target the very first time (I didn't on my first 3 attempts), but you'll be pretty close. And with practice you'll wonder how you did it any other way!

The power of the notepad (or smart phone!)...

I want to share with you something that above all that assists me more than anything else in my writing efforts - the humble notepad!

Whether it's quickly jotting down ideas that come to me when I'm out and about, or as a reminder of something I need to remember to do, it's become an invaluable tool.

I also keep one by my bed: if I come up with an idea before bed and fail to write it down, I just don't sleep. It's as if my subconscious is telling me to offload it somewhere! Once I've written it down, I sleep like a baby!

I also use it for those 'just-waking up' creative *ah-ah!* moments.

How many times have you thought of some great idea, failed to write it down, and then it's just gone from your head? Add up all those moments and think of how many ideas have passed you by!

So wherever you are and whatever you're doing, whether it's a simple reminder, a sentence you need to remember, or an action you need to take, for heaven's sake write it down!

Yes, I do realize it's the 21st century and that everyone uses smart phones now; I do too.

But I find nothing matches the immediacy of writing something down. As soon as an idea hits you just jot it down; you can even 'doodle' something as a reminder, if that's what is required.

If you're more comfortable using a smart phone then go right ahead. I have to admit I have an iPhone and sometimes use the dictation feature in the *Notes* app to quickly say an idea that comes into my head – now *that* is actually quicker than a notepad (but it can sometimes make you look a little crazy!).

Once you get into the note-taking habit, you'll never go back!

...and the To-Do list

And don't underestimate the power of the humble to-do list. There's an awful lot to think about when you're writing a book and it can sometimes feel a little overwhelming.

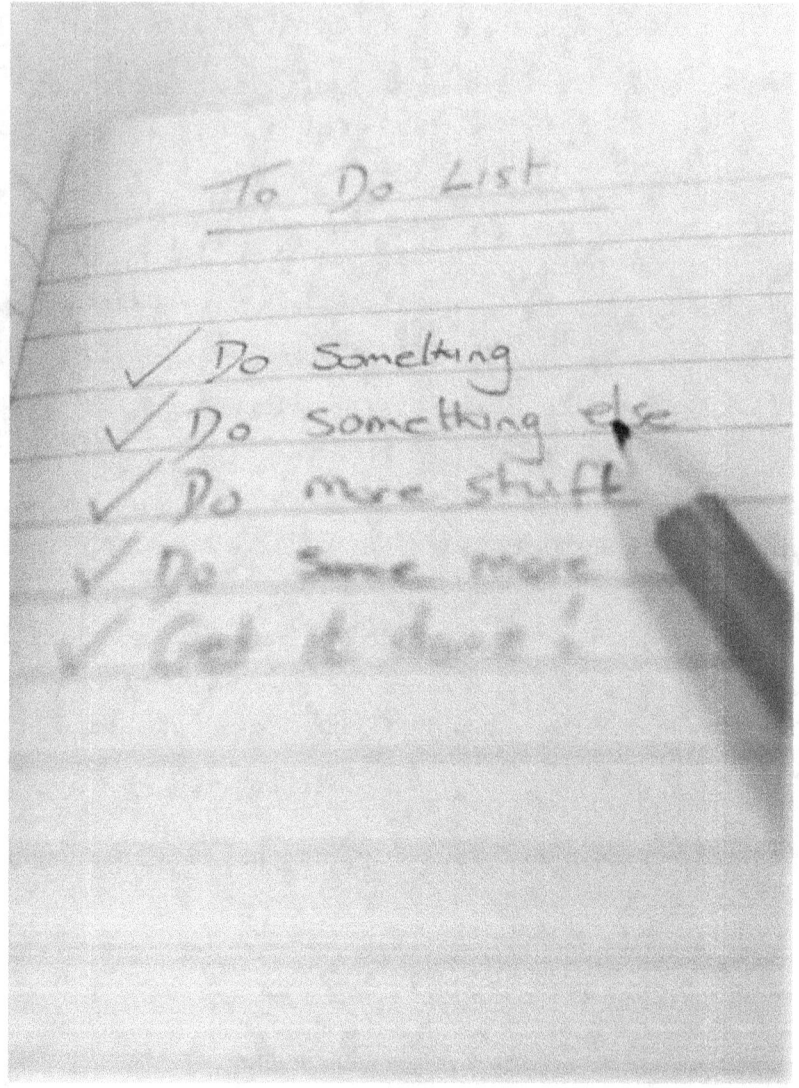

You're thinking up new ideas, considering your outline, your book cover, how to tackle the next section, considering your marketing strategy, planning your follow-up books, etc..

But fear not - this is where the humble to-do list comes to the rescue!

I simply write down all the things I need to get done. This is a very fluid list that I'm adding to and amending all the time.

Again, you can use a smart phone. But I would only ever recommend using a simple app like Notes – I've never found a time-management app that doesn't end up taking up *more* of my time!

Break things down

Then from this huge list, I'll create my daily 'to-do' tasks in my A4 day-to-page diary.

My priority is always to finish the book in hand, so an action that takes me closer to this goal must always come first on this list. But once I've completed my outline or written my 1,000 words, I may have an action to get my book cover outsourced, or run a promotion on another book.

A to-do list will help to focus your mind on what's important NOW.

By splitting your mountain of work into these small, daily to-do lists, the world becomes manageable once more.

And any tasks you don't complete, just transfer them to the following day.

Plus there's nothing more satisfying than ticking off the items when you complete them!

As well as a daily task list, at the beginning of each week I also create a separate list of 'Goals' I want to have completed by the end of the week. This might be: 'complete at least 3 chapters', or 'research x,y and z', or 'get book cover done'.

These weekly goals help you to 'keep your eyes on the prize': sometimes completing your daily goals can make you feel a little like an automaton, blindly actioning and ticking off jobs without seeing the bigger picture (liking completing your book!).

A weekly task list will keep you goal-focused and will also help spark off a list of daily tasks you need to do to complete them.

But remember: writing things down and to-do lists are extremely important, but are nothing without the most important thing you need to remember: taking action on them! No amount of to-do lists are going to write your books for you. Action is what builds momentum that makes things happen. Action leads to more ideas and more action!

How to get the most out of this book

To gain the most value from this book, I want to ask for certain commitments from you:

1. **You must have a determination to succeed as an author.** Without this, no amount of training will help. You need to WANT to succeed.

2. **Read each chapter through.** Then go back and fully action all the points covered in that chapter. You will only learn by *actively participating* in the whole process. Just skimming through the book won't work - learning is an ACTIVE process!

3. **Clear away any negative thoughts or feelings of self-doubt.** This is the time to be completely uncritical of yourself and to allow your creative side to emerge!

4. **Highlight any points you notice that are of particular interest.** You'll remember them much better if you do.

5. **And when you've completed your book and are a successful author, let me know about it!**

So first it's time to do some washing up: take all the dirty dishes out of the bowl, drain the water and fill it with warm, clean, soapy water, put on your '24-hour hat' and let's get started!

2. THE 'QUICK TURNOVER' FORMULA

I'm writing a book. I've got the page numbers done.
- Steven Wright

How can I write a book in just 24 hours?

24 hours?

Impossible I hear you say!

I'm going to go one step further: my formula will allow you to write the actual *meat* of your book (here I mean physically writing the actual chapters, with the headings, the full stops, the commas, etc..) in just 12 hours!

As a rough guide, I break the 24 hours down as follows:

- Idea Research Time – 2 hours
- Prep Time (Outlining) – 6 hours
- Writing Time – 12 hours
- Proofing Time – 2 hours
- Production Time (Publishing) – 2 hours

With every book, this mix will vary slightly depending on your knowledge of the subject and the chosen genre; with some, the research may take a little longer, with others the writing time may even take a little less and perhaps the outlining a little more.

But, using my process, I've been able to finish the majority of my books on or around the 24 hour mark.

And with practice, it just gets easier and easier!

Q. How long should your book be?

A. As long as it needs to be!

As I've alluded to previously, your audience no longer wants to read 500 page novels on the history of dieting or on the benefits of meditation.

Be honest, when was the last time you read a 500 page non-fiction book from cover to cover?

People are busy. They want fixes, not fluff. They want solutions to their problems; as quickly and as digestible as possible. In a book that's easy to both read and consume.

So the first thing you need to do is to get yourself into the mind-set of your audience. What itch do they want scratching?

Stop thinking *book*, and start thinking *solution*.

So how long should it be? There's no right or wrong answer to this as it very much depends on the niche you are targeting. If you're writing a book on the *History of Britain*, then you may struggle to complete in the allotted time. On the other hand, a children's picture book may only need a hundred words.

But as a general guideline, my view is that a good quality non-fiction information book, covering all of the RELEVANT topics need only be around 15,000 words; some maybe more, some maybe less. In other words, it needs to be of an *appropriate* length for your chosen topic.

Smaller, more specialized books also attract more reviews than the huge 'resource' books.

This doesn't need to mean sacrificing on quality.

My books are mostly around this length and I make no apologies for it: I want my books to stay punchy and to the point with absolutely zero waffle; and that address all the points on my chosen topic. But to do that I need to make sure that my books don't 'bite off more than they can chew'. In other words, make sure a topic is selected that you can completely cover, without leaving any important stuff out!

I would much prefer to read a short book that answers all my questions to a 500-page book packed with so much waffle that I don't even finish it.

And if the book does what it says on the tin and delivers on its promise, we'd all be happy to pay 3 dollars for that, wouldn't we?

My formula is broken down into the following steps:

- Getting those all-important book ideas;
- Researching and validating your ideas (a 'sense-check' if you like);
- Creating an outline of your book (where the real magic happens!);
- Writing your book;
- Proofing your book, and finally
- Publishing your book.

What you'll need

I'm not going to be too prescriptive here, but these are the tools I use and recommend:

- A PC or a Mac with word processing software installed (I use Microsoft Word, but plenty of free alternatives are available)
- A day-to-a-page diary (A4 size)
- Pack of *Post-It* notes and *Post-It* strips (available from most stationery stores)
- Mind mapping software (Xmind, FreeMind, Simplemind)
- Publishing software (Word, Calibre, Magic Bullet Books)
- Sharp Pencils
- 2 small notepads
- PC Microphone (optional)
- Headphones (optional)

You'll also need to find yourself a quiet area, free from all distractions (more on this later).

You may already have an inkling of the kind of book you want to write, but for those who don't, or who need a little sense-check, let's begin with the area that often stops people at the first hurdle: getting those all-important book ideas!

3. STEP 1: GETTING YOUR BOOK IDEAS

"Think left and think right and think low and think high. Oh, the thinks you can think up if only you try"
— Dr. Seuss

You already have a book idea. You just don't know it yet! The trick comes in coaxing it out of your subconscious!

It's no use simply waiting idly around, expecting divine intervention.

As writer Jack London put it: *"You can't wait for inspiration, you have to go after it with a club!"*

I can't tell you what you should write about. You are unique; you are made up of the sum of your own interests, hobbies, skills and experiences.

But discovering new ideas is the fun part!

You just need to get yourself into the right frame of mind, to prime your brain for action in order to recognize those opportunities.

And action always leads to more action!

Exploiting the Baader-Meinhof Phenomenon

Have you ever come across a word or phrase you've never heard before, and then over the next few days, you encounter it repeatedly?

It's a curious but actually a very common experience of synchronicity known as the 'Baader-Meinhof Phenomenon'.

It's the same with ideas and opportunities: your brain can recognize them, providing it's *primed* correctly to notice them.

And once primed, you can also take advantage of the *recency* effect, where your brain remembers the most recent information supplied to it.

So how do you do you prime yourself for action?

Well, you simply need to put all the relevant material in front of you! The material in this case is going to be all the possible areas you might want to explore for your book ideas.

But at this stage we're not actually going to be coming up with the ideas themselves, we're just priming your subconscious brain ready to begin working the magic.

Here's how:

Method 1

On an A4 piece of paper, create a 2x2 grid.

In the 4 sectors give them headings of:

- 'Work experience',
- 'Hobbies & interests',
- 'Things I know about', and

- 'Inspiring people'.

Now complete each section, as comprehensively as you can!

At this stage you need to be as loose and uncritical of yourself as you possibly can - don't discount anything, even if you think it sounds lame.

For instance, for me, I had the following under 'Work Experience:

Programmer, cocktail barman, warehouse clerk, insurance clerk, purchaser, web developer, author, internet marketer, PowerPoint compiler, IT support and bouncer!

Once you've added all you can against *work experience* and *hobbies & interests*, think what these, together with everything your life experiences, have provided you with in terms of skills and knowledge.

Put everything down, no matter how silly or insignificant it may seem. Suppress that critic inside you – if it helps, have a glass of wine to loosen you up and release that creativity. You may be surprised what comes out!

Under *inspiring people*, I wonder if you know anyone who has inspired you, either in a business or personal sense, perhaps someone who motivated you in some way? Do they have a story you could retell? Maybe you could even tap into their expertize?

Give yourself plenty of time for this stage and be as open as you can; dismiss nothing!

How many things did you come up with?

Tip: sometimes it can be hard to get into the right creative frame of mind, particularly if you're new to this process, so here's how to get yourself warmed up and more receptive:

Try making some random unrelated lists: for instance, write down as many household items beginning with the letter 'B' as you can, things you could do to improve your life, or as many jokes as you can think of. Make up some of your own.

Doing this helps to liberate your 'real' self and shuts out that internal critic, enabling that all-important creative flow. Then go back and try again. Be patient. Once the mind starts flowing, you'll find it hard to stop!

Method 2

If, after an hour, you're still racking your brain, struggling to fill that page, here's a way to add to your list:

Is there anything you've always wanted to do but never made the effort to try it? Have you always made an excuse and simply wriggled out of it? It may have been trying to lose 10 pounds, to get a six-pack, to run a half-marathon, to learn a new language?

This exercise needn't just be about writing books. It can also about changing habits, to show you that there are opportunities out there if you just go out and grab them; they aren't going to come and get you!

You need to get out of your proverbial chair and actively go searching for them! Right now, you are the potential of everything you will do for the rest of your life. You can decide right now to change your existing habits and do something different you've never done before.

How about a 30-day challenge? Why not give yourself 30 days to achieve something you've always wanted to do?

Or even go on a course on a subject you've always been interested in? I've written a good many books on the back of inspiring courses I've been on. Your book sales will more than subsidize your costs!

Keep a diary of your experiences and your struggles. Read around the subject in books, forums, magazines and add everything you learn into a diary.

Don't you think people will be interested in your story? Non-fiction books don't just need to be educational. They can be inspirational too.

Look at books like: *Run Fat Bitch Run* and *Getting past the first 30 seconds*. These are inspirational stories about average people who challenged themselves. They immersed themselves in the process and then simply shared their experiences.

Can't Swim, Can't Ride, Can't Run was about an unfit, overweight man who'd never done any exercise before and decided to take on a triathlon; and in a later book the iron-man challenge!

It's time to stop underestimating yourself and what you *believe* you're capable of!

And the great thing about this method is that by the end of the process you'll not only have a new skill, you'll also be passionate about the subject, wanting to share your trials and tribulations with the public!

"The worst enemy to creativity is self-doubt." - *Sylvia Plath*

Method 3

If you're still struggling, why not look at the latest trends on Amazon?

The 3 main areas that always sell involve:

- Health & Nutrition (How to get fit / healthier, eating well, diets, recipes);
- Wealth (How to make / save / be better with money);

- Relationships & Happiness (How to find / keep someone, how to be happier, calmer, more in control, etc..).
- Children's Books

Is there a niche in one of these areas that you can step into? Rather than writing a generic diet book, perhaps a book on 'dieting for busy moms' or 'how to make money from home'?

What problems can you solve?

There's also a whole host of fad diets around at any one time – perhaps you could put your own twist on one of these?

How about a children's facts book? These can be a great way to get started as an author; and the great thing about picture books is you don't need many words!

Browse through and drill-down into the various book categories on Amazon and see if something clicks.

< Kindle Store
< Kindle eBooks
Nonfiction
  Arts & Photography
  Biographies & Memoirs
  Business & Investing
  Children's Nonfiction
  Computers & Technology
  Cooking, Food & Wine
  Crafts, Hobbies & Home
  Education & Reference
  Health, Fitness & Dieting
  History
  Literary Criticism & Theory
  Parenting & Relationships
  Politics & Social Sciences
  Professional & Technical
  Science
  Self-Help
  Sports
  Travel

Remember, you only need to be a couple of steps ahead of your reader for someone to be interested in what you have to say. To provide your reader with inspiration or education (or both!). Scratch their itch and they'll be happy. This doesn't need to mean compromising on quality, just staying on-topic and addressing your reader's specific needs. I would be and constantly am more than happy to pay $3 for a book that can do that!

I used to be in awe of someone who could juggle – until I was able to do it myself and realized it really wasn't all that hard once I put in the practice!

Sometimes the smallest step in the right direction ends up being the biggest step of your life.

Time to Reflect

"Your mind will answer most questions if you learn to relax and wait for the answer."
William S. Burroughs

Hopefully you'll now have a completed grid and a few ideas of the kind of niches you want to focus on.

You may want to fine-tune your ideas by visiting related forums in your niche and viewing topics and reader's questions to see what areas your audience is particularly interested in (this method is also great for coming up with the sections for your book).

Write everything down, no matter how insignificant you may think it is.

OK, it's time to let all this sink in. So go away and forget about them!

Let your subconscious get to work. Don't underestimate the importance of this step (remember the *Baader-Meinhof* principle).

Go for a walk, a run, to the gym, meditate.

Tip: Keep a notepad with you wherever you go and also keep one by your bed; I find many ideas come to me just as I'm waking up. And write down everything.

I like to give myself a day or two to mull things over and for the magic to happen. Whenever something pops into my head, I write it down.

By the end of this process, you should have a list of ideas. For some it be may be ten or twenty ideas, for others, two or three.

It doesn't matter; the important thing is that you now have some ideas to start playing with!

Help, I'm still stuck!

If you've been through this entire process and tried all the methods but still have no clue what to write about, just drop me a line and I'll send you my *Top 100 Niches for 2015*. All I ask in return is for an honest review on Amazon.

These are niches which regularly get between 5,000 and a million searches per month in the US and UK!

And due to the large amount of traffic these niches attract, you only need a very small piece of the pie to be assured of many hits to your book. And you'll be surprised at just how short some of these niche books need to be and still gain insane amounts of traffic!

Again, it's all about providing a solution to people's problems.

I've had great success using this method (join my list and I'll share with you a case study I'm planning to do very soon in one of these niches).

You can also drill down into these niches if you like to make them more exclusive. There must be a niche here that takes your fancy!

"Don't think. Thinking is the enemy of creativity. It's self-conscious, and anything self-conscious is lousy. You can't try to do things. You simply must do things"
— Ray Bradbury

4. STEP 2: VALIDATING YOUR IDEAS

"Creativity is just connecting things. When you ask creative people how they did something, they feel a little guilty because they didn't really do it, the just saw something. It seemed obvious to them after a while"
– Steve Jobs

OK, it's time to sense-check your ideas.

For each idea you have, see how closely it fulfils the following criteria:

- Is it believable and credible? (i.e. It doesn't make outlandish claims you can't back up) **(1 point)**
- Does it solve a specific problem? **(1 point)**
- Does it target a specific niche/audience? **(1 point)**
- Does it lend itself to a 10,000-15,000 word book? (to cover all *relevant* topics) **(1 point)**
- Are there spin-off opportunities for your idea? (more books, hooks or angles, a brand) **(1 point)**
- Are you interested in the topic? **(1 point)**
- Is it an evergreen topic? (i.e. not something that will be outdated over time such as a Photoshop manual) **(1 point)**

- Is it unaffected by seasonal factors? (e.g. a Halloween craft book) **(1 point)**

You may have noticed that I haven't included how much competition there is as one of the questions. Competition is rarely a bad thing – it's actually a sign of a successful niche, so never be scared of competition. And armed with the right marketing strategy, you'll have no problem leap-frogging most of your competitors.

However, you do need to be mindful of not writing too generically on a subject area if there is a ton of competition, for example, "How to lose weight"!

Tip: Think of a niche/target market within the area you want to focus on. It will be easier to brand and to identify yourself as an expert in that sector e.g. weight loss recipes for busy moms. Just don't spread yourself too thin - there still needs to be a sizeable enough market to target.

Sometimes you discover the best ideas by finding out what *not* to do.

Now score each of your ideas out of a possible eight.

If your ideas score 5 or more, then they pass the test. Over 6 and you're really flying!

Discard the other ideas for now – you may want to revisit them at some later point to see if there are different approaches to the topics to make them more viable.

Creating a Brand

I'll cover this in more depth in my marketing book, but I want you to think very carefully at this point about whether you can create a *brand* on your chosen topic.

Building a brand will transform your efforts and allow you be distinct in your chosen marketplace, engender additional trust and sell more books and spin-off products.

A brand is more than just a logo and a website (but this is a good first step). It's also about providing a consistent message, providing value and communicating with your customers.

Never underestimate the power of branding.

Tip: If you do plan on writing in different genres that have absolutely no relation to each other, make sure you keep your pen names for those book separate! Amazon allows you up to 5 pen names, so use them. The last thing you want is to release a children's book and an erotica book under the same name!

Testing your audience

Now for the remaining ideas, you need to see if the target audience is large enough for your ideas to be viable, and more importantly, profitable!

To do this, go to *Amazon.com* and choose the *Books* category. I then tend to choose the *eBooks* link on the left (this link may change i.e. may not be evergreen!).

You'll then be presented by a list of categories on the left-hand side. Drill down until you've reached the section that most closely matches your genre. So in my case, I might choose:

Reference > Writing, or

Reference > Writing > Writing skills

Tip: I recommend drilling down as much as possible in order to get the most accurate idea of audience interest.

Now look at the top 5 books on the first page. If you click on each in turn, you can then scroll down to the *Product Details* section, which will display that book's *Amazon Bestsellers Rank*. This will provide a value based on its sales figures: the lower the number, the more popular the book.

Amazon Best Sellers Rank: #1,762 Paid in Kindle Store (See Top 100 Paid in Kindle Store)
#1 in Kindle Store > Kindle eBooks > Nonfiction > Self-Help > **Creativity**
#5 in Kindle Store > Kindle eBooks > Business & Money > Entrepreneurship & Small E
#14 in Books > Self-Help > **Creativity**

My general rule is that if the top 5 books on the page all have a Bestseller Rank of less than 15,000, you have yourself a successful niche!

If most are below 10,000 then things start looking even better. To give you an idea, a book with sales rank of 10,000 will be selling roughly 10 copies per day (300 copies per month); those with a sales rank of 5,000 will be averaging around 30 books per day (around 900 copies per month)!

It's estimated that a book in the top 10,000 outranks 99% of all Kindle book sales! So if your book manages to reach even 30,000, your book is going to be very successful.

Do this final test against your remaining ideas, and you'll hopefully find that a winner should magically emerge.

If you need final confirmation that your idea has legs and will be profitable, there are actually outsourcers on Fiverr.com who will research your idea and let you know the market's viability. I have used a gig occasionally in the past just to give me the extra assurances I needed.

Tip: some people never make it past this stage as they're waiting to think up 'the perfect book' that no-one has ever written before and that has a potential market of millions. Breaking news: this is unlikely to ever happen! So don't spend forever worrying that your book idea isn't good enough. If it passes the Amazon test above and gets a good sense-check score believe me, it's good enough!

Find a niche and go with it - don't choose 3 or 4 to hedge your bets. You'll risk spreading yourself too thin. Put *everything* into that one niche and get as many books as you can from that niche before moving on to the next one.

Hopefully after you've done all this, you've just nailed your winning book idea!

5. STEP 3: OUTLINING YOUR BOOK

"If you don't have time to plan, do you have time to waste?"
— Peter Turla

The Magic 'Slicing and Dicing' Outlining formula

OK, this section is perhaps the most important section of all; it's where all the magic happens!

It's going to lay the foundation of your entire book and form the basis of your entire writing efforts. Get this part right and you've nailed it!

This is where your entire book will take shape before your very eyes!

The Basic Structure

I construct all my books according to what I call my 'what, how, next' formula.

So every book will have the following pattern:

- **What** – what problem(s) are you solving? I also try to include a back-story to demonstrate a certain level of expertise and to reassure my audience. This usually involves a:

o   *Problem/Struggle/Discovery* (how I identified the same problem as my audience, what I did to research the problem/how I worked through the problem and found a solution).

- **How** - describes in detail the exact steps needed to solve their problem.

- **Next** – what are the next steps the reader needs to take after reading your book?

This is simply the 'overall' structure. What we need next is to learn how we identify the 'nitty-gritty' sections, sub-sections and actual 'outline content'.

Get Yourself Prepared

Outlining, writing and proofing your book requires a degree of discipline and concentration. But with a little pre-planning, and the right environment, it becomes pretty easy to put an hour's effort in at a time.

I'm ashamed to say that I remember, as a kid, doing all my homework in front of the TV. Because of that it probably took me 3 times longer than it should have and the resultant output was well below what I was capable of - and my early career most definitely suffered because of it!

So let's get the environment right and get ourselves organized before going any further.

What you'll need:

- A PC or laptop with your favorite word-processing software (I use Microsoft Word but any will do);
- A4 notepad and pencil;
- A pack of *Post-It* notes and *Post-It* strips;
- Mind mapping software (Xmind, Simplemind, Freemind);
- A timer of some kind.

Your environment

Where you work is an extremely important factor; get this wrong and it can have a massively negative impact on your productivity.

First you need to identify where your main work area will be.

If you're lucky you have a quiet office you can retreat to. If not, you need to seriously start thinking of somewhere you can go with a laptop. Perhaps it's a local library, a coffee shop, a bookstore, even a friend's house.

If you think there's going to be any distractions, invest in a good pair of headphones (noise-cancelling if possible) and listen to your favorite music - without lyrics preferably.

If it's at home, you may also want to alert your family/housemates that you're about to embark on a new writing adventure and that you need to set aside an hour or two day that's totally distraction-free. Just communicating with them in advance can make all the difference, and save a lot of pain for all concerned!

In my case, I've converted a room into a study area that's fully primed to be a calm, stress-free writing environment.

In my case, I make sure that:

- my desk is totally cleared of superfluous items and paperwork, leaving only my keyboard, mouse, notepad and pencil;
- I have access to music (non-vocal is the way to go – Mozart is my favorite choice. Also check out www.focusatwill.com for a great selection of tunes to write to);
- the room has good lighting (a desk lamp is ideal as it focuses your mind on your work area);
- I have a comfortable chair;
- the temperature is just right (I just can't concentrate if I'm cold);
- I pre-warn everyone in the family that I'm about to start writing and am not to be disturbed for the next hour unless the building is burning down;
- I turn off my cell phone;
- I close ALL the applications on my PC, apart from my word-processing, mind-mapping and perhaps music software;
- I've taken care of any jobs I needed to do that might distract me;
- if there are going to be distractions around (i.e. kids), I'll stick on my noise-cancelling headphones!

Identifying the main sections

So with your newly found idea, you probably have a general idea of what your book is going be about and what areas you want to cover.

But you're worried whether you're covering off all the topics and even if you have enough content to fill an entire book. You also want to make sure that each section flows from one to the next and that you're not missing anything out.

Time for a brain-dump!

Here's what I do:

I start by writing down all the possible sections/areas I want to cover on my chosen topic. I don't worry for now about getting them in the right order, whether they're even topics or even how many I write down, so don't be too critical at this point. At this stage, it's all about getting your ideas down on paper.

So for this book, I had:

- Introduction
- Outlining
- Writing
- Marketing
- Evaluating ideas / Validation
- Organizing
- Interests, hobbies
- Skills
- Note-taking, to-do lists
- Book length
- Competition
- Equipment (what you need)
- Getting ideas
- Rewards
- Inspiration ,quotes
- Topics, organizing
- Timing
- Branding
- Outsourcing
- Motivation, discipline
- Environment
- Writing software (writing, mind-mapping)
- Description and title
- Publishing (process, software)
- Proofing

- Pricing
- Reviews
- Platforms
- Resources

I then transfer these to the *Post-It* notes, writing one onto each.

Next, I arrange them on the table, trying to identify the main sections and establishing some kind of overall 'flow'.

I may find that some of the sections aren't sections at all but would fit better inside others as sub-sections (headings within a section). So I strip those out and write them on the *Post-It strips*, sticking them onto the appropriate sections where I can. Some I may even discard altogether or maybe use later in my content.

Note: Strange as it may seem, your introduction can be completed more comprehensively at the end! At this point, we're not entirely sure of the exact content, or even all of the sub-sections, only the main sections, so we don't know exactly how we want to 'present' the book to your audience in the opening chapter. You don't want to miss introducing the main content-teasers or worse still, make promises for content that doesn't even appear!

In my case I knew I wanted to give the reader an idea of how I got to this point, and why the reader should be interested in what I have to say.

So I wanted to include:

- My back story,
- The importance of writing books,
- The importance of having a solid writing formula,
- Some 'teasers' of what the book contains and what it should deliver.

I can return to it at the end and make sure I'm happy with it then!

Once I'm happy with the main sections and the order in which they flow I can then begin thinking about splitting the main sections into sub-sections.

Getting that all-important content

OK, you should now have a good idea of the main sections and the order you want to cover them in. You probably also know roughly some of the sub-sections and vaguely what you want to say in each.

But we want to make the writing process as easy as possible, don't we? We don't want to be staring at blank pages, wondering what we're going to say next!

In short, we need a plan!

The sub-sections

So select your first section and think of all the points/topics/questions you can possibly think of appropriate to that section; these are going to form your sub-sections and short 'flash'-summaries of your outline content.

For example, for this section, I wanted to cover:

- Environment

- Music distractions, other factors?

- What equipment do you need?

- What planning/outlining tools are best?

- Structure?

- How to get the book sections?

- How to fill the sections with sub-sections/content?

- What medium/software to use?

- How to get enough content?

- How to fill in any gaps?

- How to make writing process easy?

- Mind-mapping software

I then decide which of these questions/topics could form sub-sections (headings and areas) in this section. For instance, I quite liked the idea of having 'Environment' as a heading in this section - one *Post-It Strip* coming up!

The sub-sub sections (or actual content!)

Now for *Environment*, what are the important factors to consider?

So I list them:

- Music

- Distractions (email, phones, kids, noise (kids mostly!))

- Lighting

- Desk, Chair

- Temperature

- etc.

These are effectively your *sub-sub-sections* - or actual 'outline content'!

The only difference between this content and that in your finished book is that they are in 'shorthand' form. When it comes to the actual 'writing' part, you're simply expanding on them and 'fleshing' them out.

For these *sub-sub sections* I prefer to simply transfer these to a notebook rather than use more *Post-It strips* - that way I can expand on them should any new ideas/questions pop into my head (the importance of carrying a notepad with you everywhere!).

Once I'm happy I've covered off all the main areas for that section, I'll move onto the next.

Hopefully you can see the magic in what I'm doing here:

1. I'm starting with the big picture (the sections in some semblance of order), then

2. drilling down into each section to identify the sub-sections (the main headings / areas) for that section, and then

3. identifying the 'sub-sub-sections', or...outline content (in shorthand)!

And the beauty is, once you've done this for each section, you'll know at a glance that by simply expanding on your shorthand content that you'll have enough to fill your book. See it emerge from the smoke!

To create more content, just ask more questions!

What if I don't know the answers to all my questions?

Depending on your level of expertise on your chosen book topic, you may or may not have all the answers to the questions you raise.

But it's highly unlikely, (unless it's an obscure question on brain surgery!) that you're unique in ever raising these questions!

Research made Easy

Do you think there are others out there who might possibly know the answers to your question??

Before the days of Google, I remember having to trail to the library to research a problem, painstakingly trawling through dusty, mostly out-of-date tomes in the vain hope I might find some relevant nugget of information.

How lucky we are these days to have: the internet!

Using a search engine, you can find all human life out there, with boundless knowledge.

Research is now easier than ever so there's really no longer any excuse for not being able to find solutions to even the most obscure information.

Yes, there is also a lot of misinformation out there, which is where your filtering, sense-checking skills come in. And by cross-referencing answers from a variety of sources, you should be able to separate the wheat from the chaff.

The skill comes in comparing and contrasting the various materials until you have amassed enough knowledge to be able to answer your question.

If there's a question I don't know the answer to I'll research on Google, blogs, forums and books, making notes as I go. From my notes, I'll compile MY own answer!

And I don't mean copying and pasting (please don't do that!).

I prefer to think of this knowledge-gathering process more as 'standing on the shoulders of giants'!

After all, what is knowledge but that gained from learning from others?

You are unique in being the owner of the experiences you have collected in your lifetime and how you have interpreted all you have learned. In other words, you are the sum of all the knowledge you have collected.

When you 'steal' an idea, it becomes a part of you and is added to all the other knowledge you have in your head. You then combine it with what you already know and then regurgitate it in its own unique form!

Our beloved Steve Jobs and Bill Gates were past-masters at this game.

Steve Jobs famously used to pick the brains of others in his industry, adapt them slightly and then make them his own. Heck, Bill Gates 'wrote' his first operating system this way!

So let's not refer to this as stealing, let's call it 'integrating new knowledge into your existing mental framework'!

Best Places to do your Research

The main sites I use are:

* *Google* - make notes from authority sites.

* *Yahoo Answers* - pose your question and make your own notes from the best answers.

* *YouTube* - a video is a great way to learn new concepts fast.

* *Related Forums* - an absolute goldmine of information here!

A final sense-check

You may want to chop and change until you're happy with the general order and flow. The beauty of this approach is you can see at a glance the skeleton of your book.

The reason I love this method is:

1.   it allows you to fully visualize your book in its entirety,

2.   it turns the whole process into a fun re-arranging game, sort of like trying to solve a puzzle, and

3.   your book should now be relatively simple to write since you now have all the content!

And let's say you have 5 main sections (chapters), together with 5 sub-sections (headings), and 5 points to cover for each sub-section (content) - that's 125 sections to 'flesh out' - more than enough for a good quality 10,000-15,000 word book.

Mind-mapping your Framework

Once you're happy with your layout, you can now transfer this to your mind-mapping software.

Here's a section of how mine looks:

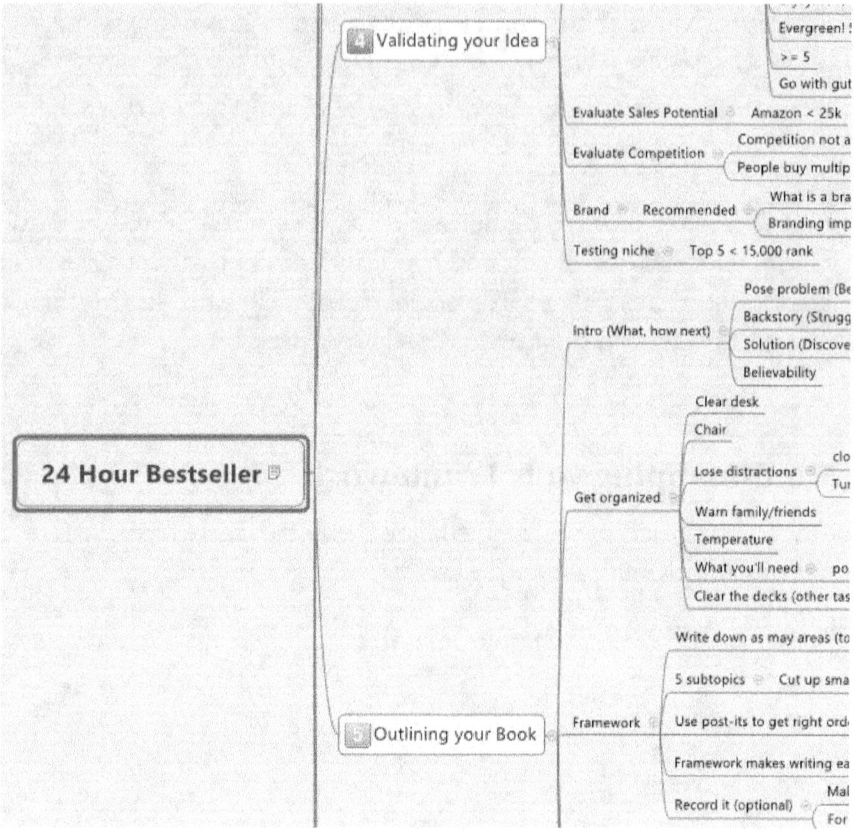

If you want a copy of this mind-map in XMind format, just drop me a line at:

james@24hourbestseller.com or visit my site at

http://www.24hourbestseller.com and I'll send it to you.

I prefer to use this linear form of layout, with the chapters in order, one below another, rather than the 'wheel' design since I think it reflects the flow of the book more realistically.

Once you've created your mind-map, run through each chapter, seeing if you want to add additional sub-sections or additional notes to make things clearer (there's nothing worse than getting to the writing stage and wondering what the heck you were trying to say!).

Talking it through

I find it also helps to talk through the book: this will often trigger new ideas/areas I want to discuss. Add them in as you go. Take notes of anything else that comes to mind.

Tip: Make sure you're completely happy with your outline before beginning the actual writing process - the more comprehensive your outline, the easier the writing stage will be.

6. STEP 4: WRITING YOUR BOOK

"How do you eat an elephant? Answer: A bite at a time."
— Children's riddle, author unknown

As an author once said, "The thing all writers do best is find ways to avoid writing."

The Writing Game

But with your comprehensive outline in place things start becoming much, much easier.

So it's time to stop treating this step as a chore and more of a challenge, even a game!

Believe it or not, this is the easy part!

Note: If you have your dictation software and you're comfortable dictating your content, you can even do it this way.

Yes, you do need to have a disciplined and hard-nosed approach. And yes, you need to sit your butt down and do a little work; but with your plan in front of you, it's simply a question breaking off a little piece at a time and going for it.

Just commit to cutting yourself off from society for 1 or 2 hours each day and getting in the zone! How many times do you just sit in front of the TV, totally bored and at a loose end? There is surely one hour you can spare each day?

Having completed your comprehensive outline in the previous chapter, this stage should no longer be a daunting prospect for you. All you need to think of doing is expanding on the points in your outline. So make sure you're entirely happy with your outline before tackling this step.

You've already done all the hard work in the outline - now you just need to break off a chunk (sub-section) at a time and expand on it.

Time is the most valuable thing a man can spend.
-Theophrastus

Break it Down

So you should now have a mind map containing your sections and sub-sections.

You should also have your notebook containing the 'outline content' for each of your sub-sections.

I like to break my writing down into 1 hour chunks (that's about the average length of my concentration span!). It should be more than possible to do 1,000 words in this time; with a little practice you might even be able to manage 2,000 (even if, like me, you can only finger-type!).

Don't worry about formatting or spelling at this stage; it will only interrupt your flow. Do all your proofing at the end.

Here's my approach:

1.   First, as with my outline, I'll remove all distractions (see 'Your Environment');

2.   I'll then open up my mind-map and drag to one side of the screen;

3.   My word-processing software I drag to the opposite side;
4.   I'll also put my notebook in front of me containing all my 'outline content';

5.   Then I'll simply choose each section in turn and start expanding on it using my notes;

6.   I'll start the timer and not take a break until the hour timer goes off. In that time I may have completed between 1,000 and 2,000 words;

7.   If I'm really feeling 'in the zone' I'll carry on. Otherwise I'll stop and check back over my work, correcting the many grammatical, spelling and readability errors (try to get used to doing this at the end as otherwise you risk interrupting your flow).

Writing Tip: If you need to write away from your normal 'base' and work on a laptop or tablet, then I highly recommend using 2 pieces of software:

Google Docs - has a simple interface, is easy to use and your work syncs seamlessly to the Cloud, and

Mind Maple mind-mapping software (works on iOS as well as on Windows).

I work on my iPad and transfer my mind map to Maple Mind and refer to this when writing in Google docs.

By making writing a habit, you'll be surprised at just how quickly your book starts coming together, even after the first couple of sessions.

Don't worry if you only get 500 words done in the first session. With practice you will get quicker.

It's important to keep your brain interested throughout this process and that you don't go 'off the boil' and become demotivated.

There's two ways I like to do this:

1. The 'word-count game'

One thing I find works for me way to do this is to challenge myself and see if I can beat my previous word count.

Before I start the timer, I'll get everything just right (see 'Your environment'), review my mind-map and visualize the areas I want to cover.

Then I'll start the timer and go for it!

If I don't meet my target, I don't beat myself up; I'll pat myself on the back for having eating through another chunk of the elephant!

Which brings me to my next strategy:

2. The 'carrot' approach

To keep your motivation levels up, it's important to give yourself rewards. For me, I'll think of a gadget I've been itching to buy.

I tell myself that once my book's published I'll buy it with a completely clear conscience - totally guilt-free! I find having a tangible reward to look forward to really keeps me focused on finishing the job.

Try to make it something positive and concrete that you can actually visualize, not just 'paying off some debts'!

You must also give yourself small rewards for completing the smaller tasks. You've just done a 1,000 word stint. Perhaps have a glass or two of wine, indulge in your favorite hobby or have a nice meal; whatever works for you.

Recognize and reward each and every achievement, no matter how small; just keep moving in a forward direction.

Now what I'm not going to do is tell you 'how' to actually write - everyone needs to develop their own style; some people like to throw in more humor, others like to play it straight. It's up to you. I try to imagine I'm talking to someone informally on a one-to-one basis, teaching and guiding them - just without the *ums* and *ers*!

One thing to keep in mind: it gets easier the more you practice!

I'm not going to lie to you - you do need to work to produce books, but by making the writing process a habit and by focusing on your successes and rewards, it needn't be a chore!

7. STEP 5: PROOFING YOUR BOOK

"I was working on the proof of one of my poems all the morning, and took out a comma. In the afternoon I put it back again."
— *Oscar Wilde*

OK, after all that writing, this is a relatively easy but extremely important stage: a badly proofed book can invite negative reviews, something you really don't want!

I categorize proofing into three areas:

1.　Spelling,
2.　Grammar and punctuation, and
3.　Readability and impact.

And all are equally important to get right.

The first is pretty straightforward: most word-processing software has a spell-check facility. Just make sure it's not trying to spell a word with a different meaning!

The second depends on how good you are at grammar. The software will only take you so far!

But the third will almost always involve a third party to 'sense-check' your work.

So read it through thoroughly, correcting as you go (I find it easier if I print it out first). Then read it through again. One author recommends actually reading it backwards, sentence by sentence, since that prevents you from assuming a sentence makes sense when it really doesn't!

Once you're happy, offer it to a friend or family member to give it a third pass.

There are also a number of third parties who can check your work for you.

One I particularly like can be found at 'Premier Proofing' (premierproofing.com).

They can really help with the 'readability' and impact of your finished work and offer suggestions on how to get your messages across more clearly. They'll provide a tailor-made quote for proofing your book.

Another way is to use Fiverr.com or Elance.com Just drop me a line if you want to know who I use to proof my books.

9. STEP 6: PUBLISHING YOUR BOOK

"Dream up a book on Monday, publish it on Friday."
- Jill Novak

Now for the *really* fun part– putting all your hard work in front of the expectant masses!

To begin with, I pretty much concentrate on publishing solely through Amazon KDP in the form of a Kindle eBook. It's estimated that Amazon account for 70% of all eBook sales – and this percentage is increasing all the time and showing no signs of slowing. For the independent author just starting out, it's really a no-brainer.

They'll also put your book in front of a worldwide audience.

Once your book is well established you may want to branch out, converting to a physical book via CreateSpace, or selling through the Apple Bookstore, Lulu, Barnes & Noble, Smashwords, etc..

But you need to give Amazon sole reseller rights in order to run free promotions of your books. So for now I'd recommend you just concentrate on Amazon KDP.

One advantage of an eBook is that it can be edited or appended easily if you notice an error too late or want to add a new section - not so easy to do with a physical book, once your reader has it in their sweaty palms!

Note: However, after perhaps a month and all wrinkles have been ironed out, I will format and submit my book to CreateSpace to create a physical book. I highly recommend you do the same: there's still a huge audience buying purely physical books.

What publishing software should I choose?

You may have your own method for publishing your books, and if it works for you then stick with it.

I use a combination of Microsoft Word and a piece of software called 'Magic Bullet Books'. It was written by an internet marketer called Brian Johnson and when you sign up to get the software, you also get tons of additional videos on how to create and market your books - it helped me a lot in the early days (remember those courses I talked about you taking?). Brian really does over-deliver with his products and the price is worth it just for the training alone.

Head over to my website for more details.

The product even includes a WordPress Author Theme that integrates with Amazon, allowing you to publicize and sell your books on your own website.

But what I love most is the actual book publishing software component itself.

It's a web-based program that takes all the effort out of the publishing process, allowing me to get on with the important stuff – like writing my next book!

| 1802 | How to Write a Book in 24 Hours (24 Hour Bestseller series) | 2015-02-27 | — Hide Pages Edit Trash |

- Copyright *(2015-03-04)* — Edit Trash
- Your Free Gift *(2015-02-04)* — Edit Trash
- Introduction *(2015-03-05)* — Edit Trash
- The 'Quick Turnover' Formula *(2015-03-04)* — Edit Trash
- Step 1: Getting your Book Ideas *(2015-03-05)* — Edit Trash
- Step 2: Validating Your Ideas *(2015-02-24)* — Edit Trash
- Step 3: Outlining Your Book *(2015-03-05)* — Edit Trash
- Step 4: Writing Your Book *(2015-02-24)* — Edit Trash
- Step 5: Proofing Your Book *(2015-02-24)* — Edit Trash
- Step 6: Publishing Your Book *(2015-03-05)* — Edit Trash
- Summary *(2015-03-04)* — Edit Trash
- Useful Resources *(2015-02-23)* — Edit Trash
- Books by James Green *(2015-02-04)* — Edit Trash

Add New Page   PUBLISH

Once logged in, you simply add your title, upload your book cover, and then copy in all the sections and sub-sections from your original document. When you're done you just click the *Publish* button and it does the rest, creating a set of files containing a .opf file, your images, table of contents and book cover.

You simply then open up the .opf file in Kindle Previewer, which creates the .mobi file which can be uploaded directly to Amazon KDP!

or...

You can, if you prefer, even outsource this entire process! There are plenty of *Fiverr* gigs who will take your documents and book cover image and convert it for you.

Marketing your Book

This is a whole topic in its own right, with a whole raft of strategies you'll need to think about from social media to building a list.

So I'll be covering this meaty topic in great detail in my next book:

24 Hour Bestseller: How to successfully market your book

But I want to get you started right away with the basics so here's the lowdown on what you'll need to cover to get your books up on the shelves and selling straightway.

Tip: I also share my top 12 marketing tips in my 'Kindle Publishing Battleplan' book, so remember to sign up for that on my website.

Your Book Cover

Never forget that you only have one opportunity to make a first impression - Natalie Massenet

Your book cover is the first thing that people see so it needs to look professional. So many people get this wrong – you only need browse through the eBooks on Amazon to see some shocking covers.

The title of your book also needs to be clearly readable – even in thumbnail form.

So unless you're a graphic designer then I would strongly recommend outsourcing this process. I tend to use a two-stage process, again using Fiverr.com:

1) First, I outsource a suitable logo of my 'brand', which is produced for me in *vector* format (this is important since it means it can be resized for various platforms without any loss of quality). This allows me to use it in a variety of ways (on my website, on Twitter, on Facebook, my signatures, etc.) as well as on my book cover.

2) Second, I use another Fiverr 'gig' to get my book cover done, sending them my vector logo in the process.

You can give your outsourcer an idea of the kind of color schemes if you want, but I prefer to just give them some examples of the kind of images/covers I like and then just let them get on with it – they're the designers after all!

And I usually find a white background works best for both the logo and the book cover.

(At the risk of repeating myself, just drop me a line if you need to know who I use to do my logo and books covers!)

Your Book Title

Amazon allows you to have a lot of characters in your book title - but don't abuse it!

Keep the main part of your title as short and snappy as you can. You can use the subtitle to expand on the book's contents. But again, don't go overboard.

So your book should ideally be in the form:

[Short and snappy title]:['this is what my book will do for you' subtitle!]

If you're stuck for an exact title, one great method is to simply start typing into Google your topic area. You'll find a ton of ideas will pop-up that you can tweak to your exact niche.

Remember, these are based on keywords your audience is already typing in! Just make sure you're not copying an existing book title exactly!

You can also use the Amazon autocomplete function to fine-tune your keywords and to see what people are physically typing in Amazon as well as how other authors are titling their books.

Kindle Store ▾	how to write|		Go

Search suggestions

Advanced Searc | **how to write** a book | dle Singl

Store : "how to | **how to write** a novel

how to write short stories

Related Sear | **how to write** short stories in 6 easy steps | ey on

how to write minutes

Apr 13, 2

how to write romance | le Lynds

how to write 10 000 words a day

how to write a book in month | k ®

how to write poetry

how to write faster

Your Book Description

After your book cover, this is the second most important 'first' impression!

This is where you need to focus on the benefits of your book, not its features. What's the difference I hear you ask?

Well, features of my book may be that it has a title, a description and five chapters; benefits on the other hand would be that it provides a repeatable formula to write your books quicker.

The more benefits you can list the more likelihood of a sale!

Feel free to take a look at my book description if you need ideas on how to craft your own description – just don't copy it completely please!

You'll see that there are headings and bullets in my description. This is done using HTML. Amazon's guidelines advise against using HTML in your book descriptions, but I believe this is because most people don't understand HTML so end up messing it up!

But the simple truth is, descriptions just look so much more eye-catching when you use HTML!

With HTML, you get to make certain sections bold, italicized, underlined, have bulleted lists, even 'Amazon-style' colored headings (woo!).

If your HTML skills are a little shaky then you're welcome to use my HTML template.

Just visit my website: http://www.24hourbestseller.com, enter your name and email address on right hand side and I'll send it to you.

Just be careful how you edit it as a <> bracket in the wrong place can cause Amazon to throw the description out.

Tip: Another great tool to test your HTML before entering it into KDP can be found here:

http://www.onlinehtmleditor.net/

It's a free tool and all done online, nothing to install.

Choosing a Book Category

You will hopefully have a general idea of what category your book will fall under. Amazon allows you to place your book into two different categories. Depending on your niche, you may want to try putting them into two completely different areas. I find the best way is simply to copy your nearest successful competitors!

As a general rule, the more you can 'drill down' your book into a smaller niche, the more chance you have of being a big fish in a small pond, rather than the other way around… but there are a few exceptions to this!

You may want to play around with the categories you've chosen and see if it has an impact on your sales.

Choosing your Keywords

You also have the opportunity to select appropriate keyword or phrases to identify your book. This step isn't too crucial so just choose small keyphrases that best describe your book.

I think mine are:

How to write a book,

How to write faster,

Book writing tips,

Advice on Writing a book and

How to write non-fiction.

Use KDP Select

KDP Select allows you to offer your book for free for 5 days per 90 day period.

I strongly recommend using the KDP Select program as it gives your book a tremendous kick-start and visibility, as well as attracting those all-important reviews.

It does, however mean that you must give Amazon exclusive rights to your book during the 90 day period. This shouldn't be a problem as Amazon are going to most likely account for 70-75% of your book sales anyway. And you can always opt-out later.

Pricing your Book

This step can make a huge difference to your initial sales and can mean the difference between getting noticed and being invisible!

My pricing strategy is as follows:

- For the first week I'll set my price-point at 99 cents for the first week, just to get it off the ground.

- I'll then put it on free promo and email my list, post on Twitter, ask my friends and family and hire my outsourcer (at Fiverr.com – yes you can ask me who I use!) to publish my book on all the major publishing outlets (and there are a lot of them!).

- After the promo I'll increase the price to a $2.99. This is the minimum price-point that pays out a 70% commission on your sales, so never go below this.

Over the following months you may want to experiment with increasing your price and seeing how it affects your sales. How much it does very much depends on your book and the niche you've chosen. There's no right and wrong answer here.

I then tend to put my books on regular *Kindle Countdown* promotions. Again, I will go into exact detail on my pricing strategies in my next book.

People love deals and if they see your book reduced by a few dollars they'll jump on it.

KDP Countdown tip: if you mark up the price of your book one week before the Countdown deal, you'll get more sales as people will feel they're getting even more of a bargain!

What I also love is that, during the Countdown Promo, Amazon still pay you a 70% commission on your sales – how cool is that?

Getting those all-important reviews

I'll cover this in detail in my next book, but you need to be thinking about getting reviews from:

- Your readers (request within your book, on your website, by email)
- Your friends and family (ask for 'honest' reviews)
- On forums (be discrete and add value first!)
- Social Media

I like my reviews to grow gradually and organically over time (I also suspect Amazon prefers to see this rather than a huge influx of reviews and then nothing!).

So don't worry about getting hundreds of reviews straight away. Most interested readers will look for social proof by the number of stars your book has and most may read perhaps the first page of reviews before making a purchasing decision.

One way to give you a big head start on is to join my closed Facebook Group at:

https://www.facebook.com/groups/kindlebookgroup/

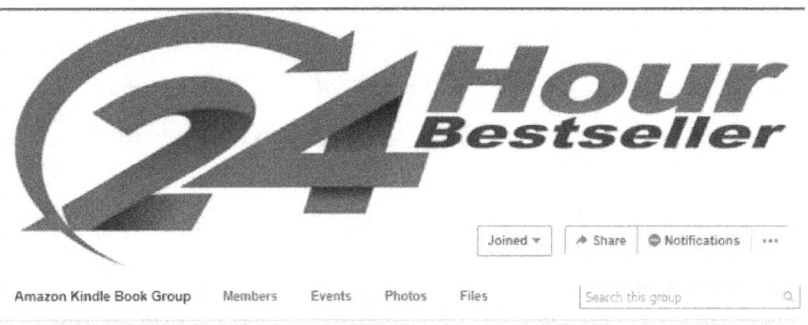

Here you can get help and advice from other like-minded authors and share honest reviews of your books with each other. The more you put into this group, the more you'll get out!

As one of my readers you'll get VIP access - all I ask in return is an honest review of my book!

Dealing with bad reviews

As Kingsley Amis once put it: *A bad review may spoil your breakfast, but you shouldn't allow it to spoil your lunch.*

No matter how good your book is, you will get bad reviews, so don't get too upset if you do. All authors get them.

Some people may not like your writing style, they may feel you haven't scratched their itch, that your book isn't long enough for them, or they may just be in a bad mood. Looking at some Amazon reviews, it really is surprising the things people find to complain about!

A bad review can feel like someone is attacking a member of your family. You might even be tempted to respond to the reviewer.

DON'T. Unless it's a valid point like it was missing a section, the formatting really is all over the place or you've simply stated a blatantly wrong fact. In which case, fix it and let the reviewer (and everyone else) politely know it's been fixed.

Respond to anything else and you run the risk of getting into a tit-for-tat argument and you will not come out of it looking like the good guy – even if you really are in the right!

So just take them on the chin and move on. That's life I'm afraid; you can't please all of the people all of the time. And don't allow their negativity to drag you down, no matter how unfair you think they're being. Just walk away!

Just make sure the bad reviews aren't down to lots of spelling or grammatical mistakes - something we refer to in the UK as 'an own goal'!

9. SUMMARY

"Someday is not a day of the week."
- Janet Dailey

I hope I've given you the tools and the kick-start you need to get up off your butt to begin that book you've always promised to write; and if you've already begun writing, the push you need to complete it.

Follow my methods and you'll very soon be a hugely successful book-making machine!

Does any of this sound familiar: you begin a new project and you get all stirred up and enthusiastic about it. But at some point you hit a hurdle and your enthusiasm starts to fade. You then start to question the value of what you are doing. You increasingly lose more interest as the project goes on and you meet more hurdles. So you move away from the project, promising yourself that you'll return to it at some point. But you never do.

Stay Positive

So it's important to keep that forward motion going. If you do come across a hurdle, deal with it head on. They only seem difficult because you've never come across them before.

Don't let them stop you from reaching your goals; they're the best learning experiences you will ever get.

Plenty of other people have overcome the same problems so reach out to others for guidance.

It's easy to come across a hurdle and then become discouraged. Don't - confront it. The next time you come across the same problem, you'll sail through. This is one of the reasons why rewarding yourself is so important. Recognize and reward each forward step you make.

Don't Aim for Perfection

Keep your mind on the prize and remember: you'll only start making money ONCE YOUR BOOK IS PUBLISHED!

Please don't spend forever wringing your hands, worrying that your book isn't perfect: no book ever is.

Or worrying that your audience will judge it too harshly: some will.

Just get it done and published. You can always tweak it later. I'll often dip into my book and add or change sections if something occurs to me later or some aspect of my book becomes outdated. This book will probably be completely different next year!

If you've followed the formula, you know the sections are coherent and have a good flow. You know there's information of value in your book. And you know you've proofed it thoroughly for errors. Enough already - publish!

Some people spend years on their books, never quite finishing them, trying to attain some weird and subjective utopian ideal of their perfect book.

Get it done, no more excuses. Make a commitment today to get started! Keep your eye on the prize.

It's time to stop procrastinating and time to start doing. *Doing* leads to more ideas – the more you do, the more you see is possible.

Give yourself the rewards along the way and recognize your achievements at each step.

And once it's out there, the fun really starts!

If Amazon likes your book and sees that it's selling and getting great reviews, they'll start promoting your books to a huge worldwide audience and also cross-promote with your new ones.

Scale it up

And when you complete that first book, don't stop there; keep that treadmill going – the more quality books you produce, the more they'll feed into each other and drive more success.

Amazon will push your first book as much as it can, but like a greedy hippo, it always wants more. This acts as a kind of validation for Amazon, that the author they've been promoting all this time, now has another great title, and another. The more you keep feeding the hippo, the more you'll be rewarded!

And the more you do, the more opportunities you'll see are possible.

Remember to think of other angles: are there spin-off books you can create from your original? Perhaps you can create a logical series of books? A subscription-based website? PDF 'cheat-sheets'?

Then there's the option of converting your books into physical books (very highly recommended), audiobooks, videos, etc.

You can even have an outsourcer convert them into other languages for you!

Don't neglect to answer your reader's questions and don't be afraid of asking them for honest feedback of your book in return.

If your book is going to be part of a brand (which I thoroughly recommend you consider creating), then I would strongly advise having a back-end website to share your ideas and your other books with a captive audience.

And always remember to keep providing value; don't cheat your audience. You need to WANT to help them.

Your book should also be something you're PROUD of, that you will gladly show to your friends and family.

Get social and start to create a buzz around any new titles you're about to release.

Create a blog using OptimizePress and get writing some thought-provoking articles.

Use outsourcers to assist you in the right areas:

- logo and book cover design
- publishing
- research
- proofing
- marketing

Get it out there, then move on to your next book! The sales of all books decline over time so it's important to keep the momentum going.

The Power of Multiples

I remember reading something that has always stuck with me:

"If you add the ages of all the occupants of a coach full of old-age pensioners, then count back that number of years, you'll reach a time before Jesus was born!"

Think about it, 30 passengers with an average age of 70: 2,100 years!

Why is that important?

Imagine you've published your book, priced at $2.99 (giving you a $2 profit) and sell 1 every day (more than achievable I'd say!). That would earn you $60 per month.

Now imagine you have 20 books published, each earning you the same.

The result?

20 x $60: £$1,200!

And that's if you're only making 1 sale on each per day!

See the power of multiples now??

Surely, using my formula, you can manage to publish 20 books in a year?

Think about creating a digital catalog business that will be an investment far into the future, rather than single stand-alone books. Start to think holistically and treat publishing like you would any business. Build a publishing empire!

And stay tuned for my next book in the 24 Hour Bestseller series: *How to Market your Book*, showing you:

- How to present your book for maximum impact;
- How to create a great back-end website;
- Branding strategies;
- How to create a marketing list;
- Social media strategies;
- Amazon pricing strategies;

- How to get lots of 5 star reviews;
- And much more.

Coming very soon – check my website for details.

And once your book's finished and for a marketing head start, don't forget to claim your free book - Kindle Publishing BattlePlan: 12 ways to sell more books on Amazon, available here.

Here's to your success and remember: you only regret the things you don't do, never the things you've done (usually!).

Know the true value of time; snatch, seize, and enjoy every moment of it. No idleness, no laziness, no procrastination: never put off till tomorrow what you can do today.
- Philip Stanhope, 4th Earl of Chesterfield

10. USEFUL RESOURCES

Recommended sites

24hoursbestseller.com – My site! Articles, advice and more.

OptimizePress.com - The only platform of choice for building your website if you want to make serious 'back-end' money from your books. Comes with full email subscriber integration for building your list, and so much more.

MailChimp.com - my favorite e-mail opt-in list subscription service.

Fiverr.com – my favorite outsourcing site.

Kdp.amazon.com – the best place to start your publishing empire!

Smashwords.com - and another.

ACX.com - turn your eBook into an audio book!

Createspace.com – for getting a physical version of your book to market.

Premierproofing.com – a great site for getting your book professionally proof-read.

GoodReads.com - part of Amazon and a great place to market your book.

Facebook.com

Twitter.com

YouTube.com

Recommended software / hardware

Microsoft Word – my choice of word processing software.

Google Docs - great if you need to write when you're out and about, or even at home!

Magic Bullet Books – my favorite Amazon book compiler. See my website for more details.

Xmind.net – my favorite mind-mapping software (free unless you want to export to other formats)

Mindmaple.com - another great mind-mapping software - and they have a version for iOS too.

Judoom.com – a 'novel' approach to word-processing!

A4 day-to-page diary.

A4 Notepad.

2 small notepads (or smart phone).

Post-it Notes and *Post-It* Strips.

Sharp Pencils!

BOOKS BY JAMES GREEN

How to Rank in Google: SEO Strategies post Panda and Penguin

How to Rank in YouTube: How to get more views on YouTube

How to Rank on Amazon : How to Self-Publish on Amazon Profitably

24 Hour Bestseller: How to Write a Non-Fiction Book in 24 Hours

Kindle Publishing Battleplan: 12 Ways to Sell More Books on Amazon

and coming very soon...

24 Hour Bestseller: How to Market a Non-Fiction Book

www.ingramcontent.com/pod-product-compliance
Lightning Source LLC
Chambersburg PA
CBHW070558290526
45790CB00002B/729